In the end, what I discovered was that, despite their considered differences—be they historic

manors, modern aeries, or the most homely and charming of farms—three things seemed

to define them all, what I have grown to call the "three essential H's" of EDEN making:

HEART, HOME, HORTICULTURE. In every case, the love of these owners

for their land and their pride in its transformation shines upon it as brightly

as a beacon. You can see it in their EYES. You can hear it in their VOICES.

And it is that same heart that takes what is merely a house on a plot of land

and invests it with the crucial emotional quality of HOME, a place of

soul-enhancing respite, consolation, and reconnection.

In the end, what I discovered was that, despite their considered differences—be they historic

manors, modern aeries, or the most homely and charming of farms—three things seemed

to define them all, what I have grown to call the "three essential H's" of EDEN making:

HEART, HOME, HORTICULTURE. In every case, the love of these owners

for their land and their pride in its transformation shines upon it as brightly

as a beacon. You can see it in their EYES. You can hear it in their VOICES.

And it is that same heart that takes what is merely a house on a plot of land

and invests it with the crucial emotional quality of HOME, a place of

soul-enhancing respite, consolation, and reconnection.

Private Edens

BEAUTIFUL COUNTRY GARDENS

Private Edens

BEAUTIFUL COUNTRY GARDENS

JACK STAUB

photographs by ROB CARDILLO

GIBBS SMITH
TO ENRICH AND INSPIRE HUMANKIND

To the owners of these ravishing Edens,
whose multiple kindnesses made this journey a true joy.

First Edition
17 16 15 14 13   5 4 3 2 1
Text © 2013 Jack Staub
Photographs © 2013 Rob Cardillo

Published by
Gibbs Smith
P.O. Box 667
Layton, Utah 84041
1.800.835.4993 orders

www.gibbs-smith.com

DESIGNED BY Michelle Farinella Design

Printed and bound in China

Gibbs Smith books are printed on either recycled, 100% post-consumer waste, FSC-certified papers or on paper produced from sustainable PEFC-certified forest/controlled wood source. Learn more at www.pefc.org.

Library of Congress Cataloging-in-Publication Data

Staub, Jack E.
  Private edens : beautiful country gardens / Jack Staub ;
photographs by Rob Cardillo. — 1st ed.
     p. cm.
  ISBN 978-1-4236-2108-9
1. Gardens—Northeastern States. 2. Gardens—Design. I. Cardillo, Rob.
II. Title. III. Title: Beautiful country gardens.
  SB466.U65.N758 2013
  635.0974—dc23
                    2012033055

CONTENTS

Preface

When I first embarked upon the notion of this book, what interested me initially was the idea that any parsing of an earthly "Eden" was, by necessity, a very individual endeavor. When one decides to surround oneself with one's unique vision of paradise, all kinds of things may come into play. Remembered or imagined images. Visceral and emotional attachments. A proclivity for water or far-flung views or snug embrace. A desire for the spontaneous or the orderly. The sound of a cock's crow or the wind through pines. The scent of lilacs. A classical bent of mind or a defiantly adventurous one.

To that end, I asked each of the garden makers represented in this book to answer some questions detailing their personal histories and the thought processes that lead them to the particular choices they made in creating their Eden. Where did they grow up? What do they work at? Did those things influence their choices? How? What first drew them to their property? How has it changed during their tenancy? What were their greatest challenges? Victories? How does opening their eyes to the morning in their Eden make them feel? How would they describe "Eden"? Whenever possible, I have used their words.

In the end, what I discovered was that, despite their considered differences—be they historic manors, modern aeries, or the most homely and charming of farms—three things seemed to define them all, what I have grown to call the "three essential H's" of Eden making: *heart, home, horticulture.*

In every case, the love of these owners for their land and their pride in its transformation shines upon it as brightly as a beacon. You can see it in their eyes. You can hear it in their voices. And it is that same heart that takes what is merely a house on a plot of land and invests it with the crucial emotional quality of "home," a place of soul-enhancing respite, consolation, and reconnection. And, finally, all of these owners are either passionate, hands-on gardeners themselves or had the wisdom to enlist the help of exactly the right garden designer to bring their unique vision of Eden to fruition.

This has been a truly lovely journey for me—physically, emotionally, spiritually. It shows what we are all capable of with a little vision and hard work, and also the infinite joys with which such an undertaking will reward us in return. I hope it will be so for you as well.

Jack Staub

Wrightstown, PA

PASSION *for* PLANTS

The first thing one sees as one loops into the drive between acres of green horse pasture threaded with the dramatic graphic of black-stained board-and-batten fences is a log and wattle ruin banked with peonies and irises and ablaze in a cloud of the most wanton of pink rambling roses. There is a careless, cottagey bravado to the gesture that, in a way, is entirely misleading, for this is no blowsy, slapdash cascading and intertwining of plant matter that awaits but, instead, an entirely disciplined if winningly exuberant homage to the best of the English garden vernacular.

The doyenne of this Anglo-Eden is a Virginia garden designer of note. She and her husband, a builder and racehorse owner, worked in concert on the property, which, when they bought it, boasted only "an amazing stand of ancient white oaks, a view of the Blue Ridge Mountains, a few fallen-down farm sheds, and a charming log house ruin. We basically had a blank slate." While he constructed the handsome Colonial Revival brick and stucco home, she set about laying the plan for the garden.

She says of this phase: "This was our third house and garden project as a couple. I had learned so much from my past gardens and knew exactly the look I wanted to create. My inspiration was surely the romantic English gardens I had visited and seen in books and magazines. The garden had to have good geometric bones with a series of linked garden rooms to create mystery and interest, and the plantings needed to be cottagey and exuberant. I envisioned flowers spilling over all the edges, at all levels, even cascading overhead. I wanted a heady fragrance everywhere and plants to attract the bees, butterflies, and birds to give the garden life."

This passionate garden maker is also a self-professed "plantaholic" and truly tireless in her pursuit of the rare and the interesting, scouring catalogues, driving hundreds of miles to visit out-of-the-way nurseries with storied stock, patiently hunting for the most interesting variegation, the most exquisitely hued blossom, the most winning bloom time or habit, and always arriving home from her excursions with an SUV laden to the rafters with plant material. The result is everything she envisioned and more.

One enters the garden off the side of the house between a pair of immense box balls that promise something wonderful beyond. To wit: a broad greensward with a central circular feature, flanked by a pair of the lushest perennial and shrub borders imaginable, these backed by a substantial hemlock hedge, crisply edged in slate, and gradating along a heady spectrum of yellows and whites to pinks and blues, then finally onto deep purples and crimsons. At the far end, a classical brick arbor clad in wisteria and pierced with a Chippendale-style central panel of teak, offers a handsomely framed window into the surrounding countryside.

An opening in the enclosing hemlock hedge to the left reveals a graveled allée of crabapples underplanted with hostas, allium, euphorbia, heucheras, and other perennials in a soft purple and blue palette with pops of variegation. From this point, the choices are diverse, as a series of grass paths winding between planting beds and shrub borders beckon one to explore what lurks just around the bend. Here, the surprise of a boulder rising as smoothly as a bald head from the center of a path provides wonderful textural contrast. There, a sculpted box topiary proves a worthy foil to surrounding planting of hostas, purple heuchera, and rhododendrons. And there, crescents of conifers, hydrangeas, and rhododendrons are enlivened with the acid foliage of a spirea and a redbud, and a border of box balls, leading the eye to a white picketed gate.

Continuing farther downslope, one's ears pick up the music of a rill and waterfall cascading naturalistically over rocks, planted with drifts of forget-me-nots, alliums, astrantia, and ferns, ultimately tumbling into a stream at the bottom of the property. Uphill to the left is a charming garden shed swathed in clematis and a cloud of climbing rose awaits near a lovely Korean dogwood. Further on is the elegant chicken house and the picket-fenced raised beds of the cutting and vegetable garden. If one drifts up towards the back of the house, one encounters a serene circular pool planted with water iris set in another green lawn, then a

beautifully conceived swimming area accented with a pillared and pedimented pool house, then, through another gate set in a wall hung with clematis and roses, a secret garden of parterre beds filled with lavender.

What is so notable about this particular vision of paradise is the beautiful balance it achieves between exuberance and order and, also, its remarkable plant palette, which, while drawing from global sources, manages to marry so fluently with this distinctly Anglo-inspired corner of the world. I'll let this ardent gardener sum it up for herself: "I love to walk around plotting and scheming new ideas and combinations. I love the opportunity to edit and constantly change. My passion is in the nurturing and designing, and even though it's often physically demanding, it is always transporting and fulfilling."

The long borders with their lovely color progression lead the

eye to a Chippendale-inspired arbor and the Blue Ridge

Mountains beyond.

True to those age-old English gardening tenets, strong axes,

enclosure, and surprise are everywhere in this garden.

Well-chosen architectural elements vie with the punch of blossom

color to provide visual and textural interest.

FEEDING *the* SOUL

She grew up on a farm in South Dakota with a passel of siblings, and attended a one-room schoolhouse down the road. They had a barnyard full of pigs, sheep, geese, beef cattle, chickens, horses, dogs, and cats, a vegetable garden and a fruit orchard that supplied their sustenance, and a self-sufficient ethos that produced milk, cheese, butter, cream, jams and jellies, pickles, and chutneys, so that they lacked for nothing and, very early on, learned the value of nature's bounty.

This lady of the land says it so well herself: "I loved growing up on a farm and living on our small farm in New York because of the daily rhythms. The crowing of the cockerel at dawn, the greeting from the cows as they are fed in the morning, the sound of the horses being led to the paddocks, and the reverse in the evening when the chickens are settling in for the night and the animals are finding shelter. As a child, when my family sat down to a meal in the summer, we would look at all the wonderful food my mother had prepared and talk with pride about how every bit of it had been grown on our farm."

She attended the local college, met her husband, married, and moved east for his job. There they first purchased an old clapboard colonial on five acres about forty-five minutes outside of New York City so he could commute to work and she could begin to reestablish some of what she had left behind in South Dakota, and they could both indulge their devotion to horses and riding. Then, twenty-five years ago, they had the opportunity to purchase one of the last great old dairy farms in their neighborhood, which had just been sold and divided into a series of capacious parcels. The one they chose boasted seven barns on fifteen acres but no house.

Their plan was to move a small colonial to somewhere on the site until a local architect convinced them to transform the largest and most prominent of the dairy barns into a home, which they did with remarkable success, girdling it with spacious porches and a Victorianesque charm. The others they refurbished into equipment and living spaces, a stable for their horses, a chicken house, a cattle shed, and a tenant house, interlinked with paddocks, pastureland, picket-fenced vegetable gardens, orchards for apples, plums, peaches, and apricots, and a few winningly conceived decorative shrub and perennial borders.

Flower gardens were never the priority in this farm girl's life, but with a new home rising out of the middle of a cow pasture, something had to be done. "We basically knew nothing. We had a shovel in one hand and *Gardening for Dummies* in the other." So she enlisted the help of her neighbor, garden designer Page Dickey, and plunged in. "And darn—it looked pretty good when we finished! By now friends had heard I was planting perennial beds, so they would send over plants as they divided in the spring. That's how the Friendship Garden around the pool was born. And I was beginning to like this flower garden thing—at least the results!"

And the results in this down-on-the-farm version of Eden are heavenly. Everywhere, there is the gift of life as guinea fowl and chickens and geese scutter underfoot and cows and horses graze peacefully in the greenness of the fields that surround the elegant cluster of barns, all painted butter yellow save for the main residence, which is a glistening white. Broad carpets of lawn are simply punctuated with rows of flowering or fruiting trees. The vegetable gardens and orchards groan with bounty, offering up squash and lettuces, potatoes, onions, chard and beetroot, fragrant bouquets of herbs, peaches and plums and apples and handfuls of blueberries, raspberries, and jewel-like currants. The eggs are fresh from the henhouse. And the only sounds are the sounds of nature: the lowing of the cattle, the trills of birdsong, the sturdy clip-clop of the horses as they cross the paddock. A perfect combination of peace and plenty.

The owner sums it up herself: "Can there be a better feeling than walking around one's garden after the day's work is done? Everyday when I ride my horse, I always finish my ride with a walk around the farm. I check the orchard, the vegetable gardens, the forest, the backside of the lilac lair. I always wonder if Thomas Jefferson felt the same joy I feel when he rode around Monticello. I can see the Hudson Highlands from the upper trail at the back of our property, and when I walk through the orchard, I always grab a peach or a plum or an apple. Later in the day, it is likely that I will take a walk around the garden rooms. I know every plant and shrub—it is like greeting old friends. Sometimes I walk with a yellow pad to make notes of what needs to be done or changed. When I am tired or weary, I leave the pad on my desk and just enjoy the peace." Surely we could all use a dose of that.

FEEDING *the* SOUL

Animals are key to the anima *of this magical property, where all of nature seems in tune.*

Fruiting shrubs and trees not only provide substantial beauty but excellent snacking opportunities along the way.

WATER FALL

This is a classic case of a high-powered couple from Manhattan who longed for a pastoral weekend retreat and got bitten by the garden bug. She is a Hong Kong–born interior designer and a retired partner at an internationally renowned architectural and design firm. He is a native New Yorker and attorney and a former partner at one of Manhattan's most prestigious law firms, where he brokered a slew of headline-making deals. Both grew up in cities that were decidedly urban and cosmopolitan, and while design was certainly in her lexicon, horticulture was decidedly not.

The home they bought, a 1960s vintage aerie cloistered in a green bower of native woodland, was not intrinsically an architectural thing of beauty, but it did have one exalted feature: a man-made watercourse that originated on the entry side of the house, ran under it, than tumbled into a series of concrete basins down a steep, boulder-strewn incline, leading the eye and ear to the shimmering presence of one of northwest Connecticut's most pristine lakes far below. In a phrase, they fell for the fall. Or at least the notion of it and the house's serene purchase on the lake.

For when this couple arrived, the fall was entirely defunct. Certainly the concrete pools and viaducts were still extant, but the workings and pipes and pumps that activated it had fallen into rude disrepair. Additionally, on this rocky, woodsy promontory, traditional garden design in terms of mixed borders, straight axes, walled rooms, or symmetrical parterre beds was not an option. This is where the strong design background and Far Eastern origins of the lady of the house came into paradisiacal play. However, first things first.

She says: "The presence of existing old trees on the property strongly dictated a shade garden. In the beginning, however, we needed to clear and clean up the land, which was full of poison oak and overgrown bushes, in order to create a path from the house down to the lakefront. The vision of the garden evolved as we formed the pathway with giant stones, creating steps and seats and garden beds along the way." A big influence was nearby Innisfree Garden in Millbrook, New York, a glory of a garden based on the Chinese garden design concept of the "cup" garden, described in the Innisfree literature as, "drawing attention to a special object segregated by establishing an enclosure around it so that it can be enjoyed without distraction. A cup garden may be an enframed meadow, a lotus pool, or a single rock covered with lichens and sedums. Streams, waterfalls, terraces, retaining walls, rocks and plants are used not only to define areas but also to establish tension or motion."

Today, after twenty years of setting things to rights, this Eastern take on Eden is a true oasis of green tranquility. Surely there is the occasional blossom in the drifts of hydrangeas and hostas, coreopsis and astilbe, but mainly this is a story of verdant texture marrying to rock and water and sky. The concrete water pools and troughs of the fall are now artfully naturalized with rock and stone. Everywhere, achingly soft drapings of moss fill stony crevasses and cloak rocky flanks. Ground covers such as pachysandra, vinca, and sedum are like lush blankets thrown over the descending hillside, wonderful in both their textural interest and their winning juxtaposition. Variegation and the punch of acid foliage add to the interplay in the leaves of various hostas lining paths. Here and there, stands of silver birch provide lovely contrast with their pale trunks and bright frills of green leaves, and ostrich, cinnamon, and Japanese painted ferns make the shadows dance with their delicate plumage.

And, always, the invigorating interweaving of the waterfall as it threads its way along paths, running underneath a stone bridge here, cascading from a rocky pool there, glistening in the dappled light of the great green canopy of the ancient trees overhead, making its way down to the lake where an Eastern-inspired teahouse-cum-boathouse provides a shady retreat along

the shore. So, as one makes one's way through the woodland, choosing this or that path to follow, inevitably, in some way, ending one's journey down by the lake, one encounters a series of beautifully executed "cupped" vignettes. A mossy stone statue of Buddha in a flurry of astilbe foliage. An immense "mountain" scholar's rock balanced on a soft carpet of moss by a weeping cherry. A circle of grass framed in river stone providing a focal point in the center of a bark pathway.

When asked what her biggest horticultural challenge was in creating her Eden, this owner immediately referenced her "own self-doubt." But "with the help of close friends, some, luckily, well-known gardeners, who provided encouragement, advice, and inspiration," she feels she was able "to bring out the soul" of this uniquely lovely spot. And the end result has been "a place where one can find peace and tranquility, where one can meditate and be in tune with one's inner spirit. A place that can also bring the same contentment and joy to others." In all this she has succeeded beautifully.

"Cupped" vignettes focus the eye inward as the gorgeous lake view beckons one to the rolling Connecticut hills and beyond.

In this garden, foliage color and form are the stars.

STEWARDS *to* HISTORY

Aldie, Virginia

The boxwoods say it all. One turns off a not insignificant state route, headed north through farm fields, some dotted with small enclaves with picturesque names featuring the major polyglot homes of the newly well-fixed, to a lane on the left one could easily mistake for yet another entrance to another such enclave. That is, until one encounters the boxwoods. Huge boxwoods. Immense boxwoods. Marching soldier-like in two serried ranks up each side, fat as tea cozies and so tall as to dwarf the car, so enclosing as to make anything ahead or to the side vanish in a cocoon of startling greenness, surmounted by a tall canopy of ancient limbs. The road is gravel and packed dirt—a real country lane, as it curves between the undulations of the green walls before looping up beside a brick edifice of truly estimable antiquity and importance.

This is a home designed by Thomas Jefferson in 1820 for James Monroe, and contains some of the earthly possessions of several other presidents and founders of this country. It houses, among other historic artifacts, the bed in which Dolley Madison escaped into dream after her beguiling days, a painted English fan in a frame with documents identifying it as the possession of Abigail Adams, and twin marble mantelpieces in the east and west parlors gifted by the heroic Marquis de Lafayette to James Monroe. It is a grand house, its Georgian pillars soaring to twenty-five feet or more, colonnaded on all four fronts, master of the 1,200 acres on which it sits.

Yet it is also a family house, the childhood home of the present owner and one in which he and his wife raised their two daughters. Two sizable yellow labs, fresh from a dip in the pond, shake and wag in greeting. The tomato teepees in the diminutive potager, enclosed on one side by James Monroe's smokehouse and his uncle's 1790 clapboard home, and on another by Monroe's icehouse, capped with a shingled nineteenth-century water cistern, are netted against the predations of the younger lab, Gus, who had just eaten the heads off a pair of lantana standards on the flagstone terrace as we arrived. Ancient trees shade splendid greenswards, and a vast complex of barns and far-flung farm tenancies dotting the surrounding pastures give testament to the property's long agrarian history through the occupancy of multiple owners through the nineteenth and twentieth centuries.

The gardens the present modern chatelaine inherited were early Jazz Age in origin, a period in which four hundred American box trees were planted to flank both the drive to the house and the spectacular axis leading from the south front of the house down through a series of broad stone terraces to a sunken circular garden at the center, then up again in a near mirror image to a half-moon gate leading into the adjacent farm fields. Off this central axis, gracious outdoor rooms radiate to right and left, defined by stone walls and green hedges, each uniquely planted in a becomingly complementary palette and designed by several hands, the last being the present owner's mother, who had been a local garden lady of distinction.

However, when the current Missus arrived, the flanking box and conifers and English ivy had so encroached on this dramatic vista that, after a rain, one could barely pass between them or even identify the fine stone hardscape underneath the overgrown mantle of green. Yet this was an inheritance with the kind of past with which one did not toy lightly. Additionally, the battery of gardeners, who historically undertook the maintenance of the gardens, were decidedly a luxury of the past. How to reconceive something so rich with history to fit the rigors of a new day? Finally, some years in, the owners had an epiphany. They would not be shackled to a past that, indeed, might have passed, but would instead be a vibrant, living part of it. So, chain saws in hand, they began to make their mark, beating back the encroaching greenery to begin to expose and lighten.

Additionally, this was not a garden suitable to the small gesture, so another answer came in adding some drifty shrub plantings to provide easy-care ballast to the borders down the long view as well as a lively shift in chroma, the extant greenery now splashed with the brilliant acid yellow of spirea goldmound and golden barberry, euphorbia and astilbe, as the deep burgundies of maples and smoke bush and purple barberry provide dramatic contrast.
In the beds, the great globular heads of purple and white allium float above swaths of silvery stachys and peonies, lilies, bearded iris, and Russian sage.

Yet here too are placid yet carefully orchestrated moments. A line of Adirondack chairs set on the great lawn to admire the views into the surrounding countryside. A finely wrought ironwork bench set against a handsome rock wall. A rustic wooden arbor shading a small gravel terrace. A charming potager in which to putter. Places for expansive family gatherings as well as small personal contemplations. A place for children and dogs with a taste for lantana. In the end, an Eden that pays graceful homage to the past while looking to the future with eyes and arms wide open.

Glimpses of surrounding architecture like this old stone

outbuilding and the nineteenth-century water cistern built atop

Monroe's icehouse add hardscape interest.

The strength of the handsome stonework in this garden marries

beautifully to the meandering encroachments of its plantings.

ONE *and* ONE MAKE ONE

Hudson, New York

The house fits so snugly into the steep, western-facing hillside that one only glimpses its roof below the protective hedge of conifers as one passes along the road above it. The owners, formerly neighbors in another New York State county, had first bonded with each other over a passion for gardening. As the male half of this couple said of their happy affliction: "We are people who, looking at a landscape, want to arrange it. We can't help it. I discreetly pull weeds in public gardens." Ten years later, they had fallen in love both with each other and, after considering a variety of possible locales, the Hudson River Valley. A view of the river was key.

However, when their realtor described the current house as a bit "ranch"-like, the couple made the sign of the cross as one would before a particularly menacing vampire and demurred. And demurred—until they had exhausted every other potential contender and were finally coaxed into tentative consideration. As they drove in for the first time, up shot their fingers in the same protective cross, for the house was everything they could have imagined and far, far less. Still, the realtor managed to herd them inside, and one look from this airy perch atop Mount Merino, where a former Livingston scion had pastured his sheep, was all it took, for the two-and-a-half-acre parcel continues to fall swiftly and steeply to the west of the house, revealing a breathtaking view of the Hudson and the Catskills across the river.

When the present owners first arrived, the anti-house was surrounded by broad expanses of asphalt for parking, a modicum of lawn, and a sea of gravel to aid in the truly problematic drainage on such an incline, which ultimately puddled in a shoe-sucking expanse of marsh at the bottom of the property. A few conifers and rhododendrons sprouted haphazardly as if seeking the only pockets of possible purchase. And then, of course, there was that house that dared not speak its name. This was clearly a property in search of its paradisiacal self.

Undaunted, the owners removed truckloads of gravel and asphalt. Drainage fields and an elaborate system of underground pipes were installed. Stone retaining walls and steps were constructed. The marsh was dredged and a second pond added. An extremely necessary deer fence now girded the bulk of the property. In the house, fenestration was improved. Arbors and pergolas were built. A gracious addition was constructed. All this in service of accentuating that enviable view and deemphasizing whatever inherent defects remained. Then, finally, the planting of their Eden could begin.

As the owner recounts, "Our topography is very demanding. Our land is steep. Some of it is very dry. Other areas weep. We have sand, clay, rocks, and not much loam. Traditional borders were not appropriate to most of our property, although we have used those techniques in places that permit them. What challenged us most and continues to challenge us is getting the plants right. Getting plants in the right place; getting the colors and textures right; getting the sizes right. It took us several years to accept the requirements of plants and to understand that wishful thinking just kills plants and wastes time."

The result has been a plant palette conceived with the expansive gesture in mind. Big stands of grasses and substantial shrubs are juxtaposed with lavish brushstrokes of perennials and ground covers covering flanks and tumbling over stone walls and down hillsides. Conifers sprawl or provide vertical punctuations. Textural and tonal pairings are ebullient and everywhere, the huge leaves of petasites providing a pretty foil to pale tufts of grass and the zing of a golden barberry as blue spruces vie with the black purple of the elderberry "Black Beauty." Elsewhere, cherry red Adirondack chairs adorn a sweeping lawn and a Luis Barragán blue arch identifies a path leading down to the ponds. A pretty teahouse, nestled in grasses,

hugs the largest pond, where a rowboat beckons. And, of course, always the backdrop of the glistening ribbon of river far below, the soft undulations of the Catskills, and the endless sky above.

This passionate gardener once again speaks for himself: "Eden to us is a place set aside from the world, a place that, once entered, shuts out all the strife, noise, ugliness, and brutality that one must accept and deal with in the world at large. We are grateful for the wondrous variety of nature, for the opportunity to have a garden, for the time and strength to tend it. Sitting in bed in the morning with coffee and plant catalogues is so much fun it is almost sinful, and there are few pleasures to equal the sun on your back while digging in good soil as your dogs play nearby." Surely it is hard to disagree.

Late afternoon light gilds the garden, illuminating

the handsome palette of conifers, grasses, and flowering shrubs.

Small internal vignettes like this fountain and archway are balanced by the glory of that jaw-dropping view.

AN EDUCATOR'S EYE

Southbury, Connecticut

One could say, I suppose, that it's all academic, but that would be a disservice to the passion of this garden maker. He has been a horticultural educator all his working life, while also morphing into a landscape designer of note, and he is also a man who has weathered enough changes in his life to not only embrace both frailty and wonder, but to rejoice in the homeliest of things: love in one's life . . . a connection to nature . . . good friends and intelligent discussion . . . love of both travel and the place you call "home."

He has been on the faculty of two fine universities, a horticultural television and radio personality, is a proud father and grandfather, and, having just turned seventy, has enjoyed the companionship of a wonderful man for the past twenty-eight years. When he moved back to his hometown in Connecticut, where he had been offered a faculty position, he purchased a small farmhouse on twenty acres of overgrown pastureland filled with invasives. There were no gardens there to speak of save for some beautiful stands of trees.

Forty years on, his passion and his expertise have had ample time to rectify that one particular void. The result is a garden that brings an entire world of horticultural knowledge and plantsmanship to this pastoral corner of the Nutmeg State. This is intelligent and aesthetic planting on every level, from the finally wrought hardscape of stonework and elegant treillage that divides and defines, to the global plant palette, to the statuary and architectural elements and admirably conceived container plantings that enliven every space. This is also decidedly

69

the garden of a plant collector. In fact, this owner says his biggest challenge has always been to integrate his one-off specimens into a pleasing whole.

This is also, marvelously, a garden that marries its farmstead provenance to a garden plan verging on something far grander. However, formality seamlessly blends with cottagey profusion here as house interiors blur into outdoor living spaces that, in turn, tease and invite the eye to move to the next garden space, then out into nature, although a nature that is fine-tuned by a master hand. The old farmhouse is the hub around which this Eden revolves. Painted a handsome gray blue with darker trim, it's a shady and serene clapboard presence as it emerges from its cloister of greenery, flagged terraces, and intimate garden spaces. Everything seems perfectly proportioned: the way the gardens relate to the house, the size of the spaces, the changes in elevation, the height of the hedges.

There are two flagged terraces, one for dining, one for repose, outside the front and back doors, populated with wrought iron furniture and the most exquisite mixed planters and groupings of potted specimens. Chartreuse frills of euphorbia spring from the dining terrace floor and pots of lavender and santolina perfume the air as one brushes by them on the way to the front door. A meandering path runs off between two undulating borders, offering an astounding assemblage of shrub and perennial specimens. From there, one is led up a granite step between two handsome trellis walls to a broad lawn flanked by box hedges and shrub, rose, and grass plantings that leads upslope in soft transition to the surrounding woodland. A classically simple pool set in a flag terrace is visible through an opening in the hedge at one end.

If one heads in the other direction from the front door, one is led down a brick path planted with a lively assortment of hostas zinged with the occasional potted fuchsia to a stately trellised seating pavilion that matches the panels to the west—a perfect spot for a shady retreat. Then, from the pavilion, stone steps continue downslope to the surprise of a pond and bog garden planted with irises and grasses and the giant leaves of petasites hidden in the dappled shade of the ancient trees that lend such a lovely air of age and continuity to the

property. And further along, in another tender moment, one is offered an enticing view of a simple native meadow dotted with bluebird boxes through an elegant garden gate, with a small grove of blue spruces and a Japanese maple providing a visual destination and a pleasing contrast to the green of the woodland beyond.

So, a water lily leaf and clematis blossom float on the surface of a Japanese porcelain goldfish bowl nestled in a border. So, in another Zen reference, a birdbath planted with a ring of moss is juxtaposed with a skirting of hosta, a Japanese birdhouse, and a burgundy-colored maple. So, the acid yellow of *Lonicera nitida* 'Baggesen's Gold' jousts with the heuchera 'Caramel' and a deep blue agave in an inspired container planting. So, two beautiful aviaries tucked into the greenery offer up a family of colorful parrots of enviable interest. I think, in the end, what is most compelling about this parsing of paradise is the fearless composer's hand this owner brings to his choices. With an entire orchestra of shrubs, perennials, annuals, tropicals, hardscape choices, garden appointments, container plantings, and potted specimens at his disposal, he interweaves his instruments with both a teacher's hand and an artist's flair.

It is the artful blending of the formal and the informal that makes this garden such a lesson in horticulture.

It's all in the details, isn't it?

LIVING ROOMS

The mistress of this particular paradise was raised on an Indiana property where horses, cattle, and corn were king, so when she moved east, a small farm where she could raise dogs, ponies, vegetables, and her children was her dream. This idyllic notion was answered in the form of an early nineteenth-century blacksmith's clapboard home on five acres outside of Washington, D.C., nestled off a former country road flanking it to the east. The property also boasted a small stable, a corncrib, the smithy, and a number of other charming work buildings in snug proximity to the house, creating a ramblingly interconnected "farmette" atmosphere every bit as winning as Marie Antoinette's. To the south, north, and west, the pastoral acreage sloped, finally rather dramatically, down a ravine to a gently running stream and, even into the late twentieth century, the property was encircled by adjacent pastureland rising steeply from the stream's far side.

However, as the former country road became a main artery into Washington and the adjacent farmland was sold to developers, unfettered and unaesthetic new housing started to encroach, topping the rises and rising from the lowlands like toadstools. Heartbreak reigned. Where others might have slunk away with their tails between their legs, these owners proved their mettle by tackling even the final insult: a thirty-room, three-story megamonstrosity hulking downslope directly to the north. And as the owners were tested almost to breaking, a new gardening philosophy was born.

Suddenly it was all about screening and enclosure, and, rather than looking upward and outward, this Eden began to look downwards and inwards, with just a peek into surrounding nature where a careful focusing of the eye would permit. Now a massive hornbeam crescent boldly encircles the great lawn to the west, effectively blocking looming development where formerly the view was tender. Now stockade fencing and white pines shield everything but the egregious megaroofline downslope to the north, and with time that, too, will disappear. And once inside this cozy paradise, one is truly transported out of time and place.

For instance, the entry drive is a stunning contrast to the now busy suburban road, layered with gas stations, fast-food joints, and new construction, that delivers you to it. Simple, well-weathered post-and-rail fences and a rural gravel drive wend briefly through a number of small, grassy paddocks as one pulls up to what was the original blacksmith's smithy, now a garage and storage building painted old-barn red and grown with a riot of wisteria and rambling roses. Bordered on the side with big stands of shrub roses and Russian sage, one of the few viewsheds left runs steeply down a slope into a pasture where an old red-painted work shed stands.

The attitude to planting is studiously blowsy and exuberant with an appealingly countrified approach to hardscape and design elements. Everywhere there are plantings and bits of whimsical architecture that combine a painter's eye and a horticulturist's lexicon with a charmingly homespun palette. Here half wine barrels planted with potatoes, chives, and snapdragons line a pathway with a diamond-paned river rock design carved in bark mulch. There a cool winter border of whites, featuring a collection of hellebores, lines a greensward with an acid green chair as its focal point.

However, it is to the north of the house, where the megamonstrosity looms close to the road and the land starts to slope first gently, then steeply down towards the ravine and stream, where a truly triumphant vision emerged. A stone retaining wall bisected by a stone stairway leads down to a sunken and leveled flagstone terrace defined on the outer boundary by a quirky slat fence and surmounted by a series of massive rustic arbors. Under one arbor, snuggled up against the retaining wall, a literal outdoor living room has been assembled with a sofa and club chairs cobbled on the property and painted an acid yellow green with blue, purple, and green cushions. Opposite, under a twin arbor, sits the outdoor dining room: a cobalt blue picnic table and benches over which floats a whimsical wirework chandelier.

If one turns to the right, up a step, one discovers a full summer kitchen housed in an open-sided, tin-roofed shed, replete with state-of-the-art appliances, giving onto the dining room and soothed by a burbling fountain fashioned from an antique mill wheel. If one climbs the stone ramp that flanks it to the right, one enters the vegetable garden tucked away behind the kitchen: an exultantly twee space of weathered raised beds with the most fantastic slat, twine, and bamboo tuteurs crafted by the owners' Nepali gardener. In the middle of it sits a rustic garden shed and arbor just big enough for a table and two chairs and perfect for some garden catalogue–leafing or a spot of afternoon tea. Truly this is an Eden that has turned encroaching misfortune into a very personal, not to say personable, triumph.

A comfy yet spirited homeliness is the defining element of this Eden.

The formal beauty of vegetables and fruits is just one of the

horticultural elements celebrated here.

SENSE *of* PLACE

One enters the drive through a pair of ancient stucco gateposts after skirting the work yards of several old farms bisected by the dirt and turf lane on which you travel. There is no marker—just a slight forking to the left between the gateposts and a continuance of the lane wending its way, up rises and down slopes, through acres of seemingly untouched pasture and woodland, with nothing but the native birds and a scattering of horses placidly grazing where the occasional paddock fence scrawls itself across a field as company. In this particular Eden, one could really be in any century, from the seventeenth on.

Finally, curving down a steepish incline between paddocks, one descends into an ancient farmyard inhabited by two impressive barns and, as the drive culminates in a circle, a fairytale dream of an ancient stone house, flanked on one side by an equally antique springhouse. There is nothing here to suggest we are inhabiting the twenty-first century, especially when one peeks into the lower barn to admire the six or so carriages that fill its ground floor, and one nearly wonders whether electricity and indoor plumbing have been introduced to this bucolic scene.

The lowest floor of the house, banked into the slope on which it sits so as to be invisible as one enters on the second floor, was built by Swedes in about 1650 on the site of an ancient and important Lenni-Lenape congress returned to that hospitable Native American tribe by William Penn in 1683. In 1750, the upper stories of the house were completed. When the current owner first saw it fifty years ago, the house was roofless and completely derelict, with cows living on the ground floor. Yet there was the peaceful seclusion and its setting on a significant bend in the historic Brandywine River, which surrounds it on three sides.

The uniqueness of this property has nothing on its owner. Renowned as both an artist and philanthropist, he is equally famous for his mischievous, carousing youth, his powerful antecedents, his immense generosity, his skill at driving a four-in-hand (which has made him an intimate of no less than the Queen of England), and the pair of Civil War–era crutches that aid him in his perambulations after too many years of brutal horsemanship and seem to invariably end up in someone's way. "I usually like to make as much trouble as possible," cautions this squire.

However, it is his passion for his corner of the world, and particularly the Brandywine Valley, where his roots are generations deep, that has ultimately defined him, Starting in 1969 with the conservation of five and a half miles of riverfront, including his acreage, the Conservancy, which he founded, has now orchestrated the conservation of an astonishing forty-four thousand acres of historic countryside in Pennsylvania and Delaware, saving it from the menacing encroachments of factories, developers, and theme parks.

Surely there are gardens here, but mainly a wish to preserve the sanctity of what has existed here since the Lenni-Lenape first chose this spot on the river for their congress. The green boughs of native woodland dappling the sun onto the water. The clouds of bluebells undercarpeting them. The morning mists that rise to reveal the mazes the owner carves in his fields to carriage in. As this remarkable figure said when asked for advice on creating one's personal paradise, "Believe and love the Eden you have and use carefully your imagination. Remember, you can't improve beauty—work with it and preserve it, so change carefully and modestly." And also, if you're the designer of this particular Eden, a wicked sense of whimsy doesn't hurt.

So an allée of hollyhocks and petunias guarded by a pair of fern-topped satyrs leads to a dome-topped yew gazebo, housing a cryptically veiled figure. A second lane of mallows leads at right angles to an African fertility bench under an arbor, featuring monkeys engaged in activities best not described here. In the circle of the drive in front of the house, a wooden statue of a dog walking a man lifting his leg—spied and purchased while journeying on a pleasure barge down the Seine in France—is proudly displayed. Or what about the sign along the entrance drive that graphically and engagingly prohibits bullshit?

These amusing eccentricities, however, are balanced by more reflective garden spaces. A cozy stone and box amphitheater garden perfect for an evening cocktail stroll or an impromptu performance. Also, the stunning early twentieth-century statue by Anna Hyatt Huntington of two greyhounds at play that decorates it. The graceful gravel trails that ribbon along the river, dappled with sunlight. And, most particularly, the splendid little stone chapel, designed by the owner, its situation a leafy bower on a rise above the river, its gothic window arches resolutely open to the elements, its only furnishings simple wooden benches and a polished chrome cross that reflects the surrounding nature as accurately as a mirror.

Passion and humor. A tender caring for what came before. A wish to leave something beautiful and generous behind. Letting Mother Nature speak for herself through you. Surely this is one definition of paradise.

As one approaches this ageless property, one nearly has the
feeling that the hand of man has passed it by entirely.

This garden owner's celebrated sense of whimsy is fully balanced by his profound dedication to historic preservation.

A NEW PERSPECTIVE

For a long time, the female half of this couple, a doctor in Manhattan, had weekended in a little clapboard house on this property, built by the previous owner in the 1960s on the land on which his great-grandfather had pastured his dairy herds. It was a house of little distinction save for one marvelous thing: it sat high on a rocky hilltop with a breathtakingly expansive view of another of northwest Connecticut's most beautiful lakes. But that, among several other key things, was about to change.

The doctor's remarriage to a recently widowed Wall Street investor prompted the decision to replace the little clapboard house with a new home that would accommodate not only their various extended families, but also the new vision of their commingled existence. To help shape this new vision, an architect who had designed another home for the investor was hired, as was landscape architect Renny Reynolds.

In order to accommodate the footprint of the spacious new dwelling, a modernist take on a Tuscan villa, the rocky top of the hill had to be dynamited, not only exposing endless yards of naked rock face above the site, but producing piles of rubble nearly as tall as the house that would replace them. Downhill, the lawn pitched steeply into a tangle of overgrown saplings, grapevines, and honeysuckle, which had grown up over time so as to obscure a good amount of the view. Still, promise was everywhere. And soon it was fulfilled.

One approaches this paradisiacal aerie by way of a pale gravel drive that snakes its way through an ancient grove of conifers and immense boulders seemingly strewn by the last glacier that carved these hills, a rock ledge rising on the uphill side as one curves towards the house. A carpet of fern and moss planted with thousands of daffodils in spring gradually gives way to lushly informal shrub and perennial plantings until one arrives in a gravel parking area

artfully divided into individual spaces by English oaks.

A long, freestanding wall with a simple opening, connecting the main residence to the guest quarters, beckons one to discover that which it conceals, which is, of course, that gasp-inspiring view. The house is anything but the predictable white clapboard that seems to populate this particular area of northwestern Connecticut. It's a rambling, barrel-roofed, stuccoed affair studded with large expanses of glass and painted in a decidedly Mediterranean palette of ochre and terra-cotta. Needless to say, this is not a structure that would cozy up to a twee cottage garden or a parading of mixed borders with much success. Such a structure begged for a garden that matched its unique personality, and the result is splendid.

Certainly there is some symmetry and classicism in the parterre beds on the lower terrace, in the handsome oval pool mirroring the lake, and surely there is adherence to those basic horticultural tenants of axis, vista, concealment, and surprise. But this is an Eden of sweep and texture and sinuousness as well as a becoming simplicity as, upslope from the house, paths wander up massive stone steps and thread their way between hefty boulders onto meandering gravel terraces. The plantings seem to emanate organically from the surrounding rocky woodland in a seamless transition from what Mother Nature has provided to what man has added.

Sweeps of hosta jostle with clouds of sedum and hydrangea, rhododendron and Russian sage, filling crevices and carpeting rock faces. Brilliant chartreuse grasses flank steps. The burgundy foliage of maples, smoke bush, and weeping copper beech provide vivid punctuations, as do the blue and green bristles of spruces and other conifers and the elegant pale trunks of a variety of birches. Here and there, carefully chosen architectural features enhance the beds. A pretty bench. A pair of antique oil jars. Up one winding path, one chances upon a charming little vegetable garden of raised mahogany beds surrounded by a twig-work fence.

Downslope, a few simple, formal elements provide a fitting platform for the house as well as a careful transition back to the native woodland below. As one stands in the opening in the long wall, a double staircase breaks an undulating hedge of purple barberry, leading one left and right down to a set of shallow, turf-faced, stone-edged steps bisected by a rill planted with a rectangle of Russian sage. These, in turn, give onto a broad gravel terrace centered on the simple oval reflecting pool, which then gives onto a sloping lawn dotted with a few stands of native birch, ending in the native tree line farther down.

Box parterre beds on the lower peastone terrace are filled with an informal luxuriance of shrub roses and perennials, and, looking back towards the house, espaliered apples provide simple green structure on the lower wall of the house. The exclamation point of a magnificent George Rickey sculpture of polished aluminum squares turns with impossibly gentle grace on itself, glistening in the sunlight. And hovering above it all is the lake far below, the gently rolling Litchfield County hills beyond, and a generous sweep of sky. Certainly something about which to exclaim.

Sky is a key element in this garden, its ever-shifting persona

reflected in the great oval pool and again in the mirror of the

lake far below.

The informality of the plantings, tucked as if by nature into

rock and gravel, give this garden a deceptively unstudied charm.

HARMONIOUS CONVERGENCE

Cockeysville, Maryland

I suppose every corner of the earth must have its own particular vision of paradise, rooted in a unique native vocabulary of flora and fauna, architectural vernacular, the reigning gods and spirits, even the quality of air and light and sun on water that could only take place in that particular place. So it is equally when two such visions commingle, creating a third that is a unique amalgam and, in a way, more singular than either of its predecessors. Such is the case with this property: an 1810 Maryland manor house, built of the softly hued local sandstone quarried on the land, set on thirty-five acres of farm pasture and forest, shaded by a trio of massive sycamores and sedately overlooking a small lake and quietly meandering stream.

He's a local boy, scion of a family who respected in equal measure the cultivation of the land and the mind and spirit. She is the eldest daughter of the monarch of the tiniest of Far Eastern states: a kingdom perched amidst the highest, whitest peaks of the Himalayas. He had cows and horses and chickens as well as a polished schooling and a love of music, the arts, literature, and foreign travel in his past; she, a childhood of almost mythic pageantry and color, palaces and monasteries clinging to the sheer flanks of snow-dusted peaks and prayer flags fluttering in the wind, leavened with a proper English lady's education.

When they wed, and he first brought her home to the Maryland countryside in which he had been raised and where he and his cousin had taken over the reins of the family business, they built a small Japanese-inspired house deep in the woods: a mossy, ferny oasis of calm. But as both aspiration and family grew, he chanced upon the nearly derelict stone house on the silted-in pond on the property on which the previous owners had planted a total of twelve trees in their forty years of occupancy. Supremely attached to their present oasis of eastern calm, she exclaimed, "You've got to be kidding!" He wasn't.

Twelve years, one thousand trees and shrubs, and some major renovation and site clearing later, an inspired union of cultures has emerged: East meets West, Maryland meets the Himalayas in the most virtuosic way. The 1810 house has become the heart of a modern home with a decidedly Eastern influence that exists in total harmony with its Western origins. Former outer walls are now inner walls, giving onto a corridor of glass that wraps around a Himalayan rock and moss garden on three sides, filling the house with light.

Further out, the plant palette is strict and decidedly Eastern in its favoring of foliage form, color, and texture over blossom, with a well-edited emphasis on conifers and maples. Certainly there are azaleas and dogwoods offering bloom and a sweeping crescent of yellow iris defining one bank of the pond, but it is really the elegant juxtaposing of blue-, green-, and chartreuse-colored yews, firs, and spruces with the acid and burgundy tones of the maples, and then the careful intermingling of rocks and statuary and swaths of gravel that define this garden. Island beds adhere to the Japanese philosophy of dry garden making, "creating a garden" being actually couched in Japanese as "setting stones upright," the stones and shaped shrubs and architectural elements mimicking mountains and streams and waterfalls, the beauty existing in the perfect balance of horizontal and vertical elements.

The result is both serene and thrilling. A graceful teahouse with a moon window crafted for moments of contemplation floats on its mirror image on the lake, a school of colorful carp swirling around it beneath the placid waters. A stone temple anchors an island of rock and conifers at the pond's center. An immense bronze elephant of Far East Indian origins gazes contemplatively out towards a native pasture. A collection of ancient stone Buddhas inhabit the crevasses of a massive and mossy rock outcropping by the stream. Brilliant courses of white prayer

flags fling their blessings into the accommodating breeze. Prayer wheels adorn columns and hang near entryways where further blessings may be cast on the house and its visitors.

As the owner so charmingly said, "Creating the garden has been in a sense like writing a tone poem. In addition to the plant material, it embraces the texture and character of water, stone, lawn, fields, and wild places. It invites the sky as an element. It is truly a garden for spring, summer, autumn, and winter as well as the seasons of a man's life." In a world in which it is the clash of cultures that seems to make the headlines, it is heartening indeed to view the harmony that can be achieved when two thoughtful minds seek to converge. This is an Eden that not only stands alone on it own terms, but offers up to us an example of what we can all achieve with a modicum of respect, partnership, and, as this owner also so accurately opined, "imagination and a little elbow grease."

The tranquil teahouse floats on its mirror image looking out to

the pastureland beyond.

Ancient Buddhas inhabit the crevasses of a massive, mossy rock outcropping by the stream.

DIVINE INSPIRATION

Washington, Connecticut

The owner of this property had once aspired to a life of monastic contemplation, with a clear eye on the rewards of heaven, before he was seduced by the very real pleasures of the here and now and, most particularly, the countless visual splendors of the terrestrial world. So, leaving the cloistered life behind, he spent a great deal of his peripatetic youth visiting the great gardens, museums, and historic sites of Europe, and especially that nursery room of horticultural inspiration, England. To say, however, that this is an English garden, although that is what he set out to replicate, would do his own creativity a disservice. This is a distinctly American parsing of an earthly paradise inspired by what is finest in the English tradition.

The property is an eighteenth-century Connecticut farmstead replete with a 1760 clapboard home, added on to over the years in a charmingly rambling fashion, and finally by the current owner with the tacking on of an ancient brick barn at the north end. One approaches the farmyard down a steep drive to a courtyard described by the house, barns, and outbuildings, situated on a pastoral thirty acres of land that continues to slope steeply down from the road to a stream, then steeply back up the opposite bank to unblemished pastureland and a forested rise. There is a gracious coziness to the situation that both reveals and embraces. When the current owner purchased the property, it had an air of graceful dilapidation about it, and was still the sort of working farm that eschewed decorative planting in favor of a packed dirt drive, some lawn, and a few shrubs and trees.

Needless to say, all that has changed with a wave of the Anglo-inspired horticultural wand. Where lawn sloped lazily down from the house to the stream, a series of handsome stone-faced terraces and steps materialized. Then hedges of box and yew and a classic brick wall to further divide the space into an intimately interconnected series of garden rooms. Then fine-looking paths of block and brick and gravel, granite-edged reflecting pools,

judiciously placed antique statuary and benches, and a charming brick garden shed. Yet there is nothing rigid about this garden and it is, in fact, the beguilingly informal formality of it that makes it such a pleasure.

For instance, the eighteenth-century farmhouse, painted a deep chocolate purple, sits in interesting juxtaposition to the two-story brick barn room now attached to it, as well as the weathered red work barns with which it shares the court. The plantings are vivaciously profuse, encroaching on pathways and spilling over walls, with plenty of volunteers allowed to self-seed, but the hardscape and green walls over which they ramble are entirely and strictly classically conceived. As one descends from room to room, down stairs and through archways, working to and fro across each terrace, one is consistently amazed at the varied personalities of the rooms, always led on by a tantalizing glimpse of what is next to come, ultimately ending in a sweep of lawn and some naturalistic but no less masterly planting bordering the stream.

One enters the garden, which falls to the south and east of the house, through a small space remarkable in its simplicity: a circular Belgian block terrace enclosed by an eighteenth-century-style fence and centered on an antique copper washing vessel filled with impatiens.

From there one descends into another serene, rather formal space, brick-floored with bracket-shaped parterre beds edged in box and planted with exclusively gray foliage and white blossom.

From there, one may drift into a garden of a decidedly different complexion: a gravel path that meanders along the stream between cheerful drifts of self-seeding oxeye daisies and *Silene armeria.* Ahead, two boxy yew sentries flank another garden entry and suddenly one finds oneself on a gracious greensward decorated on either side by a pair of astounding mixed borders beautifully edged in granite block. Here, shrubs joust with perennials and a variety of gorgeous dahlias with strong accents of burgundy and chartreuse foliage.

If one proceeds north along that terrace, one enters the walled garden, featuring a rectangular pool set in a granite terrace and protected on the north and west by a fine brick wall pierced with two arch-shaped entries and swathed in euonymous and variegated kiwi. Another exuberant border, filled with deep blues and purples and jolts of crimson and spilling riotously over this room's granite floor provides brilliant color and form between the arches. One continues north through the arches to the upper lawn and the long yellow border below the house, looking down onto the great lawn, the stream, and the untouched pastureland across it.

If our modern Edens are truly the result of a sympathetic partnership between man and nature, this garden is a marvelous example: hardscape meeting native turf in a perfect relationship, with that ever so slight friction that is the ultimate suitability. Equally suitable is the news that this garden owner and creator has just entered into an agreement with the Garden Conservancy to leave this delightful Anglo-inspired property as a fully public garden upon his demise. Even now it is open for touring on Saturdays in season. Rejoice, therefore, at another little permanent pocket of paradise preserved on earth!

Box-edged beds and rooms are one of the classic features of the Anglo gardening tradition.

Self-seeders are encouraged in this garden, softening the

exquisite hardscape with their capricious presence.

NORTHERN EXPOSURE

It is as if Moby Dick had elected to break with startling immensity through the placid ocean's surface of the lawn, his pale hump glistening. To wit: a granite rock ledge four hundred fifty feet long and forty feet tall mirroring the length of the entrance drive and nearly dwarfing the house in the distance. Surely there are other gardens on this one hundred eighty acres surrounding an 1813 clapboard home in New York State, but none that make such a *large* statement. Now scrubbed of debris, mulched with peastone, and gorgeously planted with alpines, one is forced to admit that one has really never seen anything like it.

The owners of this unique garden feature, who formerly worked at jobs in public relations and advertising in Manhattan, were simply looking for a weekend getaway. To that end, they chose this property, originally just six unkempt acres, "because of the house, which had old-age charm, the right room configuration, four fireplaces, and it was affordable. The fact that the property was overgrown and scruffy didn't concern us, because we had no interest in gardening!" The master of this Eden, who was born and raised in London proper, further elaborates that, "although I attended boarding schools in beautiful parts of the South East [of England], I managed to avoid deriving any inspiration from my environment at all."

In the beginning, he continues, "we weren't looking to surround ourselves with any vision of Eden, but rather to enhance our weekend experience. First we wanted to clean up the area around the house and make the approach more attractive, so we cleared scrub and installed a lawn and proper driveway. Later we started to think about growing our own vegetables and herbs and creating a small garden." Then the plot began to thicken.

"We began to fall under the influence of friends who gardened. On trips to visit family in England, we began to take an interest in their gardens and public gardens nearby. We then saw our own space in a more informed light and discovered features that were interesting and special. To learn more, we started taking courses at the nearby Berkshire Botanical Garden. All this culminated in a decision to hire a local landscape designer to create our first planted area. We watched him carve out the area, shape beds, amend the soil, and select plants, and we were hooked!"

However, to start, things were not always idyllic in terms of honing this vision of paradise. "Our biggest challenge was our lack of knowledge and experience of gardening, so that we kept on making elementary mistakes. We also didn't have an overall plan, so we had to find a way to connect disparate areas into some sort of coordinated whole. Another challenge, arising out of our inexperience, was the fact that we had probably bitten off more than we could chew." That would be the one hundred eighty acres they were now determined to tame.

Thirty years later, things have changed dramatically. When asked what improvements they have made to the property, the list is daunting. "1) Expanding the house, and adding a swimming pool; 2) Exposing the 450-foot-long rock ledge, cleaning it out, adding peastone mulch throughout, and planting it (fifteen years of work by hand!); 3) Doing the same to a 150-foot-long rock garden that was a smaller extension of the same ledge but completely submerged under trees and weeds; 4) Creating perennial borders around the swimming pool; 5) Transforming newly acquired land from abandoned gravel pits and second-growth woodland to meadows. 6) Converting our original vegetable and herb garden into a water garden; 7) Creating a larger and more elaborate vegetable garden, together with a barn for tools and equipment; 8) Installing a greenhouse attached to our potting shed; 9) Adding a lavender garden, a container garden of tropical plants, and a woodland garden; 10) Digging a three-acre pond."

Not too shabby for a couple of inexperienced weekenders who, initially, took no interest in gardening at all. Now, however, having happily retired from the rigors of Manhattan, horticulture is their delight and their passion. When asked to describe that idyllic ideal, the owner has this to say: "Eden is a garden paradise that stimulates the senses and is a joy to experience on every day of every season. It is the delight of looking out of any window in the house and being presented with a beautiful picture that we have had a hand in creating. It is the pleasure of walking down paths whose borders change every week, and pausing at points that offer either quiet intimacy or peaceful distant views."

And now, what of gardening? "It makes us feel connected to the environment in an active and satisfying way. It presents a constant creative challenge with huge rewards to look forward to. It places physical demands on us that keep us healthy and strong, and it offers us the opportunity to learn something new every day." And truly what could be more paradisiacal than that?

A broad circle of slate and gravel surrounding an antique sundial provides a central feature from which garden paths radiate.

Expanding one's horticultural palette to embrace unfamiliar

plant forms and families is one of the great joys of gardening.

GRACE LAND

Middleburg, Virginia

This is another property with a past. Originally part of the immense five million plus acres inherited by Thomas, Lord Fairfax, in 1719, it inhabits one of the most beautiful landscapes in America: a place of rolling pastureland and farm fields giving onto the softly hued grandeur of the Bull Run Mountains to the east and the Blue Ridge Mountains to the west. The modest stucco over stone farmhouse was built in 1790 on a rise overlooking the splendid views, and in the mid-nineteenth century was home to John W. Dodd, a member of a family of famous Southern Methodist educators.

Like most of the adjacent properties, this was a decidedly agricultural affair: a self-reliant fiefdom that produced sustenance of every description, with cattle and horses dotting the fields, chickens scurrying underfoot, and furrowed rows groaning with plenty, so a springhouse, a smokehouse, and a handsome complex of barns and work sheds were soon added in charming proximity to the house. This pastoral story, however, was about to shift personalities dramatically as the historic property entered its most intriguing chapter and the United States its darkest hour with the commencement of the Civil War.

Virginia, grown rich on its slave-based economy, seceded from the Union with the Confederacy and, eventually, saw some of that tragic war's most terrible battles. The most famous local participant was "the "Gray Ghost" himself, Colonel John S. Mosby, who, leading the 43rd Battalion of the Virginia Cavalry, known forever after as Mosby's Rangers, famously and heroically bedeviled the Union Army with his lightning-fast raids and devil-may-care cunning.

When John W. Dodd's seventeen-year-old son George joined the 43rd Battalion, the little stone house on the hill became a safe house for the Rangers. The trapdoor leading to a concealed crawl space in which the young Rangers would hide from the Union forces is still extant in the living room floor. Additionally, the scar of a cannonball fired by Union troops traveling south from Washington along what is now the drive can still be viewed on the north side of the house. After the war, following the tenancy of the Dodds, the farm remained resolutely agrarian, the house astoundingly not receiving electricity, running water, or indoor plumbing until 1955.

The current owners purchased the 130-acre farm in 1975, embracing its charming antiquity and sublime views, and, initially concentrating on the refurbishment of the buildings, did not start gardening in earnest until 1985. In the past twenty-seven years, this Eden's chatelaine, one of the leading lights of the Garden Club of Virginia, has transformed what was essentially a rustic working farm into an amazingly graceful country estate. Bowing both to the antiquity of the house and the local eighteenth-century horticultural vernacular of box-bordered beds and rooms, she has divided the spaces around the house into a series of elegant vignettes, each framed by the charming architecture of the outbuildings and each leading the eye out to the resident herds of Black Angus cattle grazing contentedly against the backdrop of the mountains.

One approaches the house down the long, sinuous drive formerly tramped by Union and Confederate soldiers, now flanked by handsome board-and-batten fences painted a sparkling white, passing a small pond, tenant house, and the stately complex of barns, these stained a dramatic black with crisp white trim and providing a handsome foil to the surrounding greenery. One glimpses the house up on the rise ahead, also painted a crisp white, through a screening of ancient trees.

If one skirts the house on the left side, one enters an enfilade of intimate garden spaces defined by the old smokehouse and box hedges broken by a pretty white picket gate leading one out into the pastureland. A small parterre bed centered on a fluted urn decorates the little court with a bursting of purple barberry and box sentinels at its corners. From there, one descends to a broad rectangle of lawn, famous for its accommodation of an annual croquet tournament, and the

long perennial border that runs parallel to the house, backed by another simple fence line with a central gate leading, again, out to the astounding views.

Up a terrace level, directly below the house, is a gracious flagged seating area, this giving onto a lushly formal graveled allée of box, azaleas, rhododendrons, and perennial plantings through a weeping yew arch, then, further down, onto another broad lawn featuring a traditional Charleston joggling board flanked by a pair of basketwork planters. If one continues around to the right, one encounters another formal boxwood parterre space with a pretty weather vane–capped garden shed as a focal point, then, further along, an elegantly spare pool enclosure. Down by the barns, a cottagey potager of raised beds decorates another courtyard.

What is most charming about this property is the timeless quality it exudes. Although the gardens are relatively new, one could easily imagine they have always existed in their current graceful form, effortlessly in tune with the antiquity and formality of eighteenth-century Virginia, and equally with the informality and beauty of the surrounding countryside and those heart-stopping vistas. In this vision of paradise, time, delightedly, stops and takes a deeply nourishing breath.

The venerable stucco over stone farmhouse played an interesting

role in the terrible conflict that was the Civil War.

Changes in hardscape like these graveled and flagged areas help provide textural interest.

REVIVAL MEETING

Originally, a modest, one-story, low-roofed home of 1950s vintage stood on the knoll overlooking the double ponds on this 40-acre property in New York State, about an hour from New York City. These, once again, were city folks with a wish for a quiet weekend retreat: he an investment guru of no small acclaim; she a well-regarded financial writer. They weekended happily in this snug, midcentury home for a good many years, bringing up their daughter, carpeting the surrounding slopes with daffodils, and carving rustic trails into the native woods, understoried with ferns and mossy boulders and boggy dells, when they weren't satisfying their yen for travel.

From the start, aside from their shared interest in the world of finance, it was their love of things classical that drew them together. They traveled extensively in Italy, Israel, Jordan, and Greece, marveling at the ruins of Pompeii and Jerash and Caesarea, relishing the perfect proportions of the Vitruvian aesthetic, and allowing the extant traces of the classical world to hone their personal vision of paradise.

So, some time in, with the help of Parisian architects Patrick Naggar and Terese Carpenter, they made the decision to replace their modest home with the house of their dreams: a building really not so much Classical Revival as truly Classical; a virtual temple to their love of the antique world, or even a marvelous ghost of one, as it now sits like the soft gray spirit of classicism on that green knoll above the ponds. The question was how to meld this monument to perfect proportion into the surrounding naturalistic landscape. To help them solve that issue, they employed the services of the classically trained landscape designer Patrick Chasse, who started to work with them and their architects even as the plans for the new house were being drawn.

The result is a series of classically inspired formal gardens that girdle the front and sides of the house, hidden as surprises in groves of conifers accessed by meandering stone steps. An oval and exuberant perennial border, anchored by French nineteenth-century herm sculptures of the four seasons, reveals itself in one green room. An "amphitheater" of clipped arborvitae on axis to the front door of the house, populated with nineteen classical busts of the likes of Zeus, Jean-Jacques Rousseau, Julius Caesar, Socrates, Nietzsche, the Duke of Wellington, and Napoleon, surrounds a sixteenth-century Italian wellhead.

To the south of the house, a bluestone terrace gives onto a severely architectural rectangular pool with a shady, classically inspired arbor along one side, a stunningly surprising stony nymphaeum below it skylit through a circular water window at the pool's end, and another oculus in the interior of the grotto allowing one to peer into the depths of the pool. Off the northern elevation of the house, an outsized chessboard is whimsically set in the terrace, this then giving onto a green room containing a classical maze of sheared yew.

This formality on three sides is beautifully balanced on the west side of the house, where a simple green carpet of lawn studded with the occasional ancient tree runs down from the pillared and pedimented gray ghost of a house to the naturalistic silhouettes of the ponds and the rustic trails and arcadian wood beyond. A nineteenth-century stone-columned tempietto containing a statue of the young Eros crowns a tiny island accessed by stepping-stones from the shore of the largest pond. In spring, the entire woodland, sloping up to the west and down to a bog on the south, is the home of hundreds of thousands of daffodils. In summer, it is all fern and moss, native trees, shrubs, and perennial plantings with rustic walkways, bridges, and stiles threading their way through the felty bog, invigorated here and there with the surprise of statuary like the ancient Chinese temple guardian standing sentry along a woodland path.

It's the way the enclosing hedges of yew and hemlock and holly meet so convincingly with the surrounding forest and lawn that is one aspect of this Eden's winning ways. The way the formal gardens are revealed in informal ways: off meandering stone paths, through the thickly planted groves of conifers. The way the new native plantings in the woodland have been added in a fashion so naturalistic one could only assume that the gods themselves had placed them there. Then, everywhere, the careful population of the garden spaces with the most enviable of garden structures and statuary and an effortless, calming, truly arcadian passage that interweaves the efforts of both man and nature into a splendid piece of whole cloth.

The oversized chess set off the northern front provides a witty foil to the classical solemnity of the house.

Features like this twig bench and potted banana add interest to

the woodland.

In the amphitheater, one has the distinct impression one is on

display for the amusement of the distinguished audience.

AN AMERICAN STORY

It all began in August 1979, when, after combing Bucks County, Pennsylvania, for more than a year for a suitable country retreat at which to establish a garden, the well-known event-designer half of this couple and his realtor plunged into the secret little valley for the first time. The designer swears he sat bolt upright and his breath stopped. For there it was: this wonderful, sad, magical, dejected place with the stream and waterfall cascading through. The classic eighteenth-century stone house. The magnificent circa 1860 dairy barns. The splendid isolation.

However, in the same nonbreath there was also the overwhelming disrepair of the place: the two huge barns crying out for refurbishment, the outbuildings collapsing, the ponds silted in with saplings as thick as wrists sprouting from the resulting bog. Each of the roofs of the two barns had holes in them big enough around to drop a large dog through, and their second-floor floorboards were so rotted as to be virtually untraversable. The carriage house, corncrib, and miniature milk barn by the curve in the driveway, all charming, vaguely Victorian structures, were superfluous to the previous owners and therefore, if anything, in a worse state of repair.

The property began as an original William Penn land grant of 1697 and had been owned by the same industrious Quaker family until 1918, its zenith occurring in 1790 when it was a prosperous 300-acre estate. However, by 1918 fortunes had changed and the last of the family to inhabit the property was forced to sell the then 185-acre homestead. Finally, in 1933, during the Great Depression, the fortunes of the farm hit rock bottom and the property, by then so derelict it was known locally as "Skunk Hollow," was sold at sheriff's sale for $370.91. Multiple owners subsequently tried to make a go of it with varying degrees of success, but by the time the present owners arrived in 1979, the farm had been reduced to 15 acres and a state of notable disrepair.

There were no gardens to begin with, but there was that astounding, historical architecture: a little village of house and barns and work buildings set above the creek and pond around which gardens could be begun. They started by dredging the pond, shoring up the outbuildings, and acquiring, finally, three more adjacent parcels of land to reconstitute 100 acres of the original property. Sets of stone steps were inserted in the rise above the house and stone terraces below it, then two broad perennial borders stretching out into a former cow pasture. A fanciful slatted gazebo was constructed to float on the now-dredged pond.

Now, thirty-two years in, the owners have shifted gears entirely. From Manhattan-based professionals in search of a weekend getaway, they have changed both their lives and careers. They moved permanently to the farm ten years ago. The event designer has gone back to his landscape architect roots and exclusively designs gardens for others in search of pastoral retreats. The former advertising executive now writes of gardens and, particularly, vegetable gardening. Both lecture enthusiastically and broadly about garden design and the saga of their garden making. They have never looked back.

If you visited this quintessentially American Eden today, you would find a total of twenty-four separate gardens on 30 of the reassembled 100 acres, the rest being given over to meadow and woodland. The woodland walk boasts a bevy of specimen magnolias, snowy drifts of 'Delaware Valley White' azaleas, a "bluebell lake," and over a hundred thousand bulbs in spring. The brilliant yellow garden at the heart of the woodland is dedicated to yellow and variegated foliage plants. The French garden on the slope above the pond is a formal parterre arrangement of box-edged beds surrounding a replica of the Eiffel Tower and encircled by rose hoops and snowball viburnums.

On the rise above the house sits an elaborate picket-fenced vegetable garden with another formal arrangement of raised beds and wonderfully whimsical permanent tuteurs capped with 1920s topiary forms. A lily garden hugs one side of the former corncrib, now home to exotic pheasants. Herb parterres and a medieval-style knot garden built on the stone foundation of an old outbuilding sit near the former carriage shed turned chicken house. Uphill are the trellis-walled "edible rooms," now permanently planted with hardy kiwi and magnolia vine, and an exotic fruit border.

The perennial borders lead out to the visual destination of a stunning circular pool garden set in a broad lawn. Upslope from that are the summer borders, planted in a hot palette of reds and purples and yellows, which in turn lead up to the pine and dogwood allée and the urn garden at the highest point of the property, featuring a twenty-foot urn on a stone plinth. Down a meandering grass path flanked by golden rain trees and a purple barberry border is the Beth Chatto–inspired Mediterranean gravel garden encircled with variegated weigela and centered on a village fountain.

Now rejoice because you can, in fact, visit. In season, this Eden is now open to the public two days a week for all to enjoy, and with the help of the Garden Conservancy, will eventually become a fully public garden in perpetuity.

Bulbs like alliums and Spanish bluebells are just part of the

glorious show in spring.

Structures like the fanciful slatted lake house and the

nineteenth-century milk barn by the drive are the anchors

around which the gardens were created.

FAMILY CONNECTION

Any life is full of sea changes and this one is no exception. What makes it exceptional, however, is the passion, wisdom, humor, and generosity of spirit that continues to propel it. She was the daughter of a prominent East Coast family, growing up in a circa 1850 farmhouse outside New York City surrounded by ancient chestnuts. When she married the scion of another well-known family and pillar of Manhattan's Catholic community, they bought a large white clapboard farmhouse, also surrounded by chestnuts, on 50 acres just down the country lane from her present house, and there they joyously brought up their brood of nine children.

Things were not always rosy, however. One daughter died tragically young and her husband saw some trying business reversals in his lifetime. Yet her indominitable optimism and energy remained unchanged even as her husband died too young as well. For a number of years she rattled around alone in the rambling home she had inhabited for fifty-two years. Then, as she entered her seventies, both sorrow and opportunity presented themselves when her dear friend and next-door neighbor died and her converted barn home on ten acres, literally and contiguously right down the road, came up for sale. And, at the same moment, after four years of widowhood, she fell in love and married another pillar of the Catholic community, a widowed geologist and local philanthropist with six children of his own. Together, they had a combined family of fourteen children, forty-six grandchildren, and, at last count, four great-grandchildren. And so they set about the planning of their dream home.

She says of this time: "As much as I loved our old house, there were too many outbuildings, etc., to manage and I thought it time to buy that ten contiguous acres. It was one of my best ideas!" And so it was. They sold the big house, tore down the barn structure on the newly

purchased acreage, and constructed a sublime gift of a house. A serene one-storied affair of native stone with barn ceilings and sunny eyebrow windows and ranks of French doors leading onto flagged terraces and broad expanses of lawn, anchored to the landscape by walls and stairways of the same native stone.

What is so captivating about this vision of Eden is not only its exceptional marriage of aesthetics and manageability, but the "inside/outside" nature of the house and garden, with the French doors flung open on all sides and its nearly immediate connection with the surrounding countryside. Surely there are a few formalesque gardens in snug proximity to the house, particularly the beautifully conceived "medallion" kitchen garden that runs down one side of the house, carved into the slope and protected by a handsome stone retaining wall. A single slate path runs under a series of rose arches with box-edged planting beds accented with box balls flanking it on each side, heading to the visual destination of an ancient oil jar: the perfect-sized potager for a household of two.

The other garden spaces, however, while described by a number of laudable hardscape choices that wed them both to the landscape and the house, are just this side of naturalized, looking as if the hands of both man and God had had equal sway. Great swaths of *Rhus aromatica* and

English bluebells carpet the entry to the house. A crescent border of azaleas, purple smoke bush, ferns, and deep blue salvia enlivened with dogwoods leads the eye seamlessly into the native woodland beyond and to the hidden surprise of a charming little grandchildren's playhouse. Downhill from the house, fairytale drifts of primulas and brawny explosions of skunk cabbage flank a meandering path of log sections through an enchanting bog garden.

Two years ago, after fifteen wonderful years of marriage, this indominitable spirit lost her beloved second husband. Yet the young sparkle is still there in her blue eyes, as well as the sense of wonder and joy she finds in the home and garden they created together. She says of it: "It's small enough for me to manage—when I am in the house, I am in the garden, and when I'm in the garden, I'm in the house." When

asked how that makes her feel, she smiles and comments, "Safe, cozy, peaceful," then begins to enumerate the very specific things that bring her those feelings: "Nature . . . snowfalls in the winter . . . new growth poking through the warming earth . . . spring . . . walking barefoot on the lawn at night in summer . . . the brilliance of fall." And finally, when asked what she might pass along to a neophyte gardener: "Follow your heart and know that a garden is never finished—thank heaven!"

Simple dry-stacked walls and sweeps of naturalized plantings

seamlessly marry the gardens to the greater landscape.

Paths echo the personalities of the garden spaces through

which they travel, as here in the bog and vegetable gardens.

One must never underestimate the decorative quality of lettuces.

MANOR REBORN

Orange, Virginia

This must be what earth looks like from Mount Olympus. Or heaven. Not so vast a height that features are dwarfed and indistinct—a map view of hill and dale. Rather, a view that manages to embrace as it reveals its expanse: valleys and pasture flanks of startling greenness, dotted with ponds and grazing horses and cattle, embroidered with fencing, receding in soft undulations to the smoky ocean tones and gentle peaks of the Blue Ridge Mountains to the west and the distant flats of tidewater Virginia to the east.

A considerably imposing Georgian Revival home of 1930s vintage sits near the crest of the promontory on which it is built, the second highest spot in all of Orange County, Virginia, encircled by a ring of two-hundred-year-old tulip poplars bespeaking the more antique home that originally existed on the site. Ditto the hundred-year-old allée of box that leads west from the house, opening onto a series of garden rooms before ascending to a trellised garden room and a very discreet swimming pool with the same transcendent view.

This avid gardening couple spent the first three years of their residency retooling the interior of the house to their needs and taste. Then they turned their attentions to the garden. As the owner succinctly put it, "Our challenge was to create gardens that reflected and enhanced the setting of a magnificent house. A great house is not really complete without equally magnificent surroundings, and we saw the site as the opportunity to create a really important garden. Our three years of ownership gave us the opportunity to make well-researched garden tours of England, France, and Italy, each of whose gardens have a distinctive flavor and each of which inspired us in our garden plan—fountains and water tricks from Italy, parterres and massed color from France, and the incredible changing color of a mixed border from England."

Together with the Virginia-based landscape designer Charles Stick, they then embarked on the creation of a truly formal wonder of an Eden. First hardscape and bones. Again,

to quote the owner: "We added structure, terracing (a Moorish-inspired gazebo, wooden and steel arbors, pavilions and pergolas, as well as water features and, of course, sculpture), and thousands of boxwood, yew, Leyland cypress, holly, and, of course, an incredible variety of plant material." The result is a dazzling series of allées, green-walled rooms, and carefully focused vistas, rigorously architectural, handsomely ornamented, and, as in all truly successful gardens, always offering anticipation and surprise as the eye is teased and led, and always with the play of water never far from ear's reach.

Although there are many ways to access this garden, the preferred entrance is up a short flight of flag steps from the gravel car park flanked handsomely by curvaceous brick balustrades and pillars topped with lead baskets and cockerels, with a lead statue of Mercury in a cloud of variegated box as a focal point. From there, one enters a series of small rooms displaying intricately knotted parterre beds, these then giving onto the grand allée of box and yew leading, in the distance, to a circular yew-walled room centered on a statue of Eros, bow in hand, on a slim column standing on paving indicating the four points of the globe. At the end of that axis, one reaches the room with pergolas giving onto the swimming pool and

an ebullient blue and yellow border. Off each side are further green rooms, some big enough

for a wedding tent, accented with glorious mixed borders and, especially to the north, giving

onto that spectacular view.

From there, one can descend an
alternate set of eastbound flagged,
brick-trimmed steps to an octagonal
water feature and massive rose pergola,
leading further downslope to the north
to two mirror-image rose gardens
featuring Chinese Chippendale–inspired
trellised gazebos and circular pools with
jets. Statues of the four seasons flank a
lawn and the northerly directed
staircases. But it is down one further
flight of steps to the north that one

achieves the final majesty of this Eden: a simple but vast circular pool with plumes of water

jetting into the air set in a broad box-edged circular lawn giving onto an absolutely jaw-

dropping view of the surrounding countryside and a handsome equestrian barn far below.

The owner provides the last word: "The marvelous aspect of a garden is the changes and

challenges it brings each season. Each week color changes and we mourn the loss of one

plant until the next season or year, and each week we glory and exalt as another plant, tree,

flower, or bush produces new foliage and color. We are constantly cutting, pruning, weeding,

planting, watering, fertilizing, and although I will not pretend I enjoy every minute, if on

balance the garden didn't provide unbelievable pleasure and nourishment to our bodies,

minds, and souls, we wouldn't be here."

Well-chosen antique garden appointments like this statue of

Eros and urn imbue this garden with an enviable richness of

character.

Exceptional roses are one of this garden's many gifts.

This garden is a superb example of how garden structure both

informs and enhances plant material.

ONE WOMAN,
ONE WILDERNESS

Bedford Hills, New York

Thirty-six years ago, a young couple from Illinois purchased an 1830 farmhouse on not quite an acre of land separated from a fairly main intersection of country roads by a tall picket fence in the charming and prosperous village of Bedford Hills, New York. From that leafy, suburban outpost, he began what was to become a distinguished law career in New York City, while she, at least to begin with, was content to raise their children and keep the home fires burning. About fifteen years in, the 6.5-acre parcel behind them, which included the two dairy barns originally connected to the farmhouse, came up for sale, and they promptly purchased it. And so a singular passion for and vision of Eden was born.

She was horticulturally unschooled, although she believed she had inherited a long-buried love of gardening and plants from her Illinoisan father, and simply plunged in, matching her husband's urban interest in the intricacies of trusts and estates with her own newly discovered, decidedly countrified passion for plants and garden making. She admits to countless mistakes, backtracking, and hard lessons, pausing to expound that she believed every plant in her garden had been moved at least three times.

The narrow, now 7.5-acre property falls gently at first from the road, from house to barn number one, then further downslope to barn number two, then far more rapidly over the bulk of the acreage to a bog and dammed-up river pond at the bottom, with the property line hugging the drive and house to the east and the greatest gardenable real estate flanking the buildings and dropping to the pond on the western side. There had been a makeshift

Monet-inspired garden adjacent to one of the repurposed barns, replete with lily pond, as the prior owner had been an artist, but the long, steep slope down to the pond, then a bog filled with saplings was an impenetrable thicket of brambles, grapevine, bittersweet, honeysuckle, and multiflora rose. Faced with the overwhelming ability of nature to thwart and even erase the paltry efforts of man, she became a woman with a mission.

First came large swaths of hardscape: retaining walls and pathways and beautiful trellised walls imported from England dividing the upper acreage surrounding the house and barns into a series of more intimate, formal rooms, further enhanced with hedges of box and yew. Then, to the west, sinuous, intensively planted beds of shrubs and perennials wending their way around crescents of lawn, revealing entrances to hidden gardens in which lily ponds and cascades of water beckoned the ear and the eye.

To the east of the barns, where the property broadens slightly in that direction, a notably decorative kitchen and cutting garden appeared: a pattern of raised beds set in a gravel terrace defined by handsome trellised walls and surrounding a low fountain, each bed boasting a beautifully planted urn or substantial tuteur at its center. Then, sharing the southern wall of the potager and down a terrace level, a state-of-the-art croquet lawn with a classical pavilion set upon a refined stone pad and surrounded with the same handsome trellised walls. This formality then transitions further downslope to shrub borders and more naturalistic plantings of ferns and hosta, then to great drifts of native meadow plants enlivened with swaths of scarlet bee balm under a canopy of native woodland, threaded through with a network of bark paths. A sense of whimsy is allowed to enter here as one chooses a path and chances upon bits of found art and unexpected sculpture.

Here a series of lacquered roots extend their gnarled arms like the sculptural wraiths of the woodland. There a stegosaurus composed of massive, gravity defying stones ambles along a trail. So, as one descends this shady, naturalized slope, looping and threading one's way through the web of paths, discovering charming vignettes along the way, one finally arrives at a garden of an entirely different personality: the bog and pond garden. A rustic chair sits

contentedly beneath a weeping willow. Reeds and grasses crowd the banks of a placid pond,

giving swiftly onto dense native woodland that looks, with the exception of a hint of a

pathway along the near bank, as
if it has never seen the hand of
man. This is far from the truth,
as our intrepid guide, the lady of
the house and equally intrepid
garden maker, shares with us the
history of the backbreaking
dredging and hauling, clearing
and uprooting that was necessary
to create this appearance of
total naturalness.

In the end, what is most

surprising about this hand-crafted garden is, first, the sheer determination of the owner

to have her way with a plot of land that seemed equally determined to strew obstacles in

her path, including, at least at the beginning, her own lack of horticultural grounding. And

second, the multiple personalities she managed to evoke on a scant 6 acres as one moves from

the refined formality of the vegetable garden and croquet lawn to the exuberant sweeps and

gushing water features of the perennial beds and garden rooms to the naturalized calm of the

woodland to the nearly prehistoric enchantment of the bog garden. One is really forced to

say, "Well done!"

*Imported English trellising, arbors, and doorways add classical
definition to this garden's spaces.*

Her lack of horticultural schooling aside, this garden owner has truly mastered the art of winning pairings and unexpected juxtaposition.

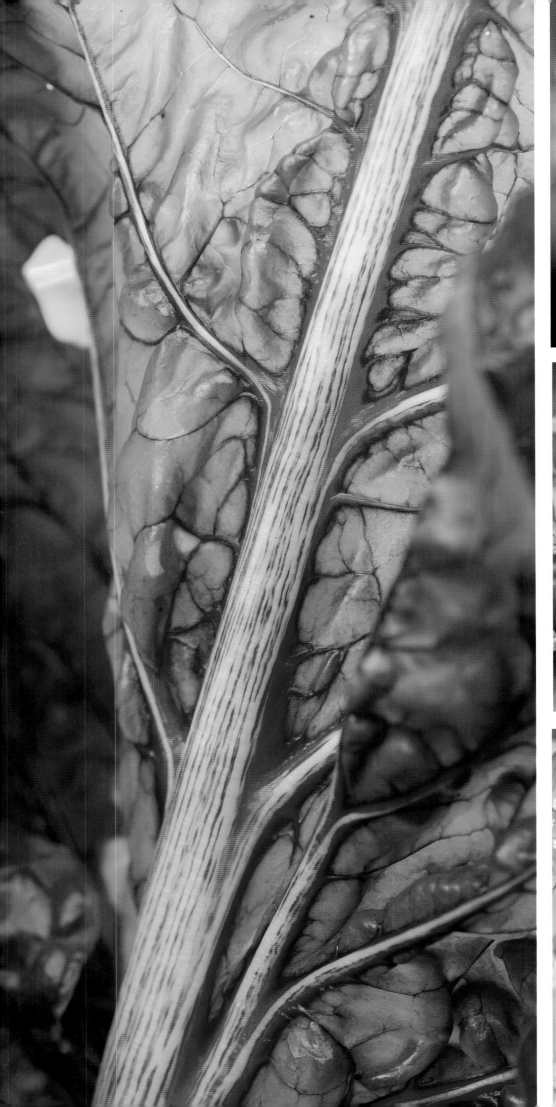

PILGRIM'S PROGRESS

She was a Cambridge, Massachusetts–based Hollywood screenwriter who bought this property, formerly owned by the widow of a world-famous pianist, as a weekend retreat sixteen years ago. What drew her to it initially was "the character of the old farmhouse, built in 1811, the 8 acres of dormant farmland that promised to be a good romping ground for my dog," and its graceful purchase on the scenic Housatonic River. He arrived some years later to manage the local Gilded Age hotel his family had purchased, but, following their conjoining, now farms their land and sells estimable produce to the local farmers markets and restaurants. They have a family of two chocolate poodles, a henhouse full of chickens, and three miniature donkeys.

She says of the property: "Over the years we have added outbuildings: an outdoor summer bedroom, a fenced vegetable garden, a wood-fired bake oven, a greenhouse, an outdoor shower, a new barn for the farm equipment, and a paddock for our donkeys. . . . And gardens everywhere."

She continues ruminatively about her horticultural tutelage: "At first, I just wanted my hands in the dirt. For the first nine years I just planted things willy-nilly. Then I went into a period of more intense study and, at the end of this period, I ripped out huge stretches of lawn, all my early work, and planted a garden from a more cohesive plan. I was a bit insane, driven by some need. Actually, the 'need' was to bring a sense of order to my immediate world when the bigger world seemed increasingly chaotic. So, while I was not setting out to make 'Eden,' it was in a way a nervous reaction to the world—environmental, geopolitical, interpersonal—around me."

Then, as she finally achieved her vision, she had a dramatic change of heart. "What had seemed 'exuberant!' like a joy suddenly seemed 'exuberant' . . . like a migraine. I was trapped by a monster I had created: I was a slave to my perennials." Salvation came in the form of a book in which she caught a glimpse of Nicole de Vesian's famous clipped green wonder of a garden in Provence. "Once again I ripped out my garden—but this time it was more like a religious experience; a quasi-insane moment of ecstasy."

The result is a very personal paradise that is as homey as it is explosive. Grass and gravel paths meander through great, curvaceous beds of riotous foliage—blues and burgundies and acid yellows—anchored by the substantial ballast of box balls and conifer cones of yew and juniper. The former garage, now rechristened the "garagerie" with the addition of skylights, is a studio/greenhouse/guest room with a four-poster bed plopped amidst the greenery. Blazingly white sheets flutter on an old-fashioned laundry line nearby. A mosquito-netted summer bedroom sits out in the middle of the upper field. Vegetables destined for the local markets march in rustic rows and inhabit plastic-sheathed hoop houses down in the lower field by the river, near where the donkeys graze contentedly in their paddock. As the sun begins to set, the dogs frolic on the lawn as the wood-fired oven on the terrace beside the house begins to blaze, ready to receive the steaks for dinner. A just-picked summer salad awaits as well. All seems, well . . . just as it should be.

This writer and gardener eloquently sums it up: "In a way, writing screenplays and gardening are similar: both require a vision of something that does not exist. Both require hours—if not years—of careful tedium to hone a craft and create the vision seen only in the mind. Both require editing and reworking, and can leave the creator adrift, without a knowledge of where to go next, but keep with the task long enough and the road out becomes apparent. The garden I have now is my 'Eden.' But I couldn't have found it unless I went through all the other work and introspection. It is a garden of less, not more. It is quiet and simpler." But, let me add, not without some defiant residual vivacity.

When asked about her definition of "Eden," she turns ruminative again: "It is a state of mind that allows one to feel safe enough to find inspiration in the universe. It is an oasis away from the noise of modern life. It is safe, meaning it is not ostentatious; it is humbly built and reveals the comforting patina of the gardener's own two hands. The paths are crooked and made of the stones that came from the beds. It is the antithesis of 'landscaping.'"

She continues philosophically about her circuitous horticultural journey: "The garden inspires me to observe carefully, because our season is short and every day is precious. There is a lovely comforting rhythm to the work—each day, and within the bigger context of the season. After more than a decade working the same land I feel both empowered (I created this?) and humbled (I don't control it); nourished by the light and the beauty but always aware that one day I will be gone and it will be given over to the inevitable, unknowable thicket of the future."

Sometimes a little rustic homeliness is just the ticket.

And often the simply utilitarian has a beauty all its own.

MEADOW LARK

Bethlehem, Pennsylvania

This 170-acre property on a country road in Pennsylvania's Saucon Valley began its existence as part of a substantial eighteenth-century farmstead. However, with the advent of the iron-making industry in this part of the Greater Lehigh Valley in the mid-nineteenth century, it was the hematite ore deposits discovered in the farm fields that became of increasing interest, and soon after its inception in 1861, the Bethlehem Iron Company, predecessor of the Bethlehem Steel Corporation, began several mining operations in the area.

After 1904, when Bethlehem Steel was founded, this pastoral corner of Pennsylvania with its rolling farmland became the building site of choice for some of that company's top executives, one of whom renovated the old farmstead and began dairy and poultry farming on a large scale. In the 1950s, the farm was ultimately sold to Bethlehem Steel itself, which subdivided the more than 1,000-acre estate to create a world-class golf course as well as several substantial building lots, including this one.

An old farm tenancy did exist on this expansive Eden, and the stateliest oaks imaginable still march in ranks down the lane to the house. One is given a key to the personality of this garden as soon as one enters the drive, which is flanked by architectural patches of golden ragwort, a wildflower rarely seen anywhere but in a native meadow. And, as one drops sinuously down to a sprawling postmodern barn complex of a home, it is the twin meadows alive with blossom flanking you on either side that begin to unlock the unique beauty of this garden.

The house, a series of barnlike structures in stone and timber connected by breezeways and pergolas around a cobbled court, seems to sit squarely in the middle of the property. As one descends to a turnabout in front of the house, low dry-stacked walls hugging the drive and echoing the house's stonework define island beds filled with a dense riot of native plants. The same exuberant native plant matter, about 3 acres in all, surrounds the house on all four elevations. As one circles the house, a gracious flagged patio, then pool area, fall in terraces from the rear of it, then the land continues to fall away to a breathtaking view of the old farm fields now populated with the same floriferous meadow plants.

Surely there are newly planted stands and sweeps of shrubs and trees. Hawthorns. Hickories. Tupelos. Magnolias. Bottlebrush buckeye. Azaleas. Serviceberry. Hydrangeas. And ranks of ancient hedgerow trees still divide the extensive farm fields below the house into a series of pastures. But where they were once the grazing fields of dairy herds, as in the front acreage, now they are triumphant examples of meadow planting. One can only imagine that it was Mother Nature herself who plucked handfuls of wildflower seeds from the sack slung over her shoulder and, in a sweeping gesture, broadcast them as far as the eye could see.

Anyone who has ever attempted a meadow knows, however, that there is nothing cavalier in its creation. This owner had the wisdom to consult with Larry Weaner Landscape Associates, who specialize in meadow planting. Management in the first three years of establishment is crucial. In this case, according to Mr. Weaner, management of the beds closest to the house are "80 percent hand of man and 20 percent hand of nature." This balance then transitions outwards to perhaps a "50/50" relationship, then out into the meadows, which are "20 percent hand of man and 80 percent nature."

Their methodology is both simple and complex. The fields are first cleared of invasive natives, then drill-seeded (as opposed to plowing, which would stir up the invasive seeds in the soil) with a perennial wildflower seed mix customized for that specific site, soil type, and climate. The first year the meadow is cut every six weeks to a height of four to six inches to allow the perennial flowers to establish below the blades of the mower, then in the second year invasive weed monitoring and removal in the establishing perennials is of the essence. By the third year the perennial flowers should be sufficiently snugly established to keep the invasives from finding a toehold.

So here on nearly 35 acres of meadow, there are over a hundred different varieties of native perennial wildflowers competing for one's attention. Coneflower, rudbeckia, and phlox jostle with native aster, amsonia, and senecio. Solidago, columbine, and the wonderful purple-foliaged penstemon 'Husker Red' vie for space with tradescantia, spigelia, and heliopsis. Aruncus, allium, and monarda cozy up to  substantial stands of liatris, mertensia, and chelone. Angelica, Virginia mountain mint, and baptisia are complemented with the feathery azure tones of big and little bluestem grasses.

The effect is beyond colorful and lush—it's dazzling. It's truly as if Mother Nature had rushed in on a floriferous tidal wave with an ocean of colorful meadow, the froth of headiest blossom crashing up against the walls of the house. And, while surely showing the guidance of a human hand, this is really her show: "Stand back and look at what I can do all by myself!"

Early morning light illuminates the splendor of this inspired

meadow planting.

Mother Nature's sense of architecture is every bit as striking as that of man.

There is little doubt that wildflower forms and foliage can be as decorative as their more highly esteemed hybridized cousins.

DEVELOPING INTEREST

St. Davids, Pennsylvania

As one drives along a meandering country road on the Main Line outside of Philadelphia, one passes a real anomaly of a house set high on a slope above a pastoral greensward dotted with two ponds. In this particular neck of the Pennsylvania woods, the greatest number of homes, old and new, are of a traditional clapboard and fieldstone personality. Not this one. For surely this is a boy's-eye view of heaven with a modernist twist: a spectacular Zen tree fort of a home on 2.5 steeply terraced acres overlooking an idyllic 20 acres of preserved open space below.

The owner, a local realtor and developer, specializes in the purchase and subdivision of some of the noble early twentieth-century estates that still populate the region, and this property is no exception. The old mansion still exists on one secluded lot along with the fifty-nine other homes that populate the 100-acre parcel. The developer retained the two most auspicious lots for himself and, defying the local vernacular, built a soaring edifice of pale stucco, lead-coated copper, and glass in a style as severe and uncompromising as a schoolmarm's rod.

Needless to say, this demanded a highly original garden, and to that end this owner wisely sought out the pioneering landscape design firm of Stephen Stimson Associates. Their goal, according to their literature, is "to create enduring, innovative landscapes" characterized "by minimalism and a modern aesthetic," with their designs being defined by "an elegant simplicity which is reinforced by careful attention to materials and detailing."

The result is a marriage made, well . . . in paradise. As the owner explains, the greatest challenge in the construction of both house and garden were the 20 to 25 percent grades along the property, a feature that made for splendid views but unique problems in the development of usable exterior space. Stimson Associates solved the problems by constructing a series of retaining walls and terraces linked by stairways that fall to each side of the house, then below it. Bluestone and teak were the materials of choice and the results are fantastic.

Massive walls of stacked bluestone slabs contain and define, giving onto rigidly linear sets of bluestone steps, which lead one from one stone and teak terrace to another. The pitch is so steep and the house so tall that one enters on the second floor and it seems as if one could step out of any room on any level onto a terrace. If all this sounds a little "cool" in personality, it gets even cooler. For, in this vision of Eden, there is water everywhere, built into the hardscape as integrally as the bluestone.

Here a rill crowns the top of a wall, then spouts into a square, river rock–filled pool below. There a swimming pool creates a waterfall at its infinity edge that cascades down the face of another massive bluestone wall, then into a grate to be recirculated. And there a rectangular reflecting pool is fed by a series of jets sprouting from the bluestone slab retaining wall above it. One feels as though it is all interconnected: a single flow of water moving from space to space, falling here, filling there, always moving, reflecting the sky and the canopy of greenery overhead.

The planting palette is as strictly limited as the architectural choices. Ancient trees that were part of the original estate landscape plan in the 1930s surround the property, a thick grove of pines girdling it on the uphill side and a mammoth black walnut extending its graceful limbs downslope, truly giving the house the aspect of being built in the treetops.

As one enters the property, pairs of river birch stand sentry in rectangular beds piercing the simplicity of a green lawn. Dense geometrical patches of pachysandra frame walkways and edge terraces. Strict rectangles of box and yew create a green interest that mirrors the austere architecture of the home and hardscape. Handsome ceramic pots arranged in groupings and

filled with tropicals and exotics add color and texture. A small potager emulates the greater garden with bluestone-edged beds and ranks of zinc planters.

Hovering above the pool, an immense wall of glass is all that separates the master bedroom's state-of-the-art shower from the sky and the leafy embrace of the black walnut. Sleek bronze sculptures and carefully chosen furniture populate the outdoor spaces in perfect complement. Massive rain chains add interest as they descend from the eaves of the house into circular concrete cisterns filled with black river rock.

What is most thrilling about this modernist Eden is the way it feels completely private while existing in the midst of a sixty-home community and commanding such remarkable views across the open space and ponds to the road below it. And, also, the fidelity of every choice and detail to this owner's unique vision.

And how does the owner feel about the paradisiacal result? "I find it very peaceful and a wonderful place to relax, think, entertain, and simply enjoy with friends and family." And finally, his words of wisdom in developing one's own Eden: "Have a vision and use the best professionals that you can find." Sound advice from a man who has definitely achieved his.

The ancient black walnut downslope of the house truly gives the illusion of living in the treetops.

Blossom is used sparingly in this garden, adding an occasional

jolt of color to the severity of the geometric greenery.

Teak panels and doorways provide a warm contrast to the

severity of the bluestone walls and terraces.